A Life of Balance

"It is good that you grasp one thing and also not let go of the other; for the one who fears God comes forth with both of them."

Ecclesiastes 7:18, NASB

a life
of balance

K.P. Yohannan

BOOKS

a division of Gospel for Asia

www.gfa.org

A Life of Balance
© 2003 by K.P. Yohannan
All rights reserved.

ISBN: 978-1-59589-012-2

Published by gfa books, a division of Gospel for Asia
1116 St. Thomas Way, Wills Point, TX 75169 USA
phone: (800) 946-2742

Printed in the United States of America

For information about other materials, visit our web site:
www.gfa.org

5th printing, 2015

To my dear daughter Sarah.
Thank you for your desire to serve our Lord.
I am proud of you.

Table of Contents

Introduction

One of my happiest times growing up in India was playing along the river. When the monsoon season came and brought the floods, the river near my village would swell. You could be sure all little kids were out on the rushing water playing in our tiny, homemade canoes—so small they could hold only one person. I was there too, just a young boy, maybe five or six years old.

Just imagine, a young little kid, no more than 60 pounds, tossing on the rushing waters of a flooded river in a makeshift canoe. I can remember countless times when the whole thing would be flipped over by the force of the water, and I'd be underneath with that canoe over my head.

But after many monsoon seasons and many flips, I became an expert at handling my little canoe in the floodwaters. I became so good that I could actually stand and put one foot on each side of the canoe and balance myself on the outer edges. Then I'd maneuver myself right through those waters. These memories make me wish I were young again.

It was growing up by the river that I first began to learn the lesson of balance, which affects life every day, no matter where we are. In order to maintain a healthy life and ministry that doesn't just come and go but is continually sustained by God and His grace, we need to have a balanced foundation in our thinking and our service. Then we will be able to maneuver safely through all that comes our way because we will be grounded by the Word of God.

CHAPTER ONE

Both Sides of the Coin

Have you ever seen those people in the circus—the tightrope walkers on the high wire? It's all balance. They must study and learn the proper way to carry themselves as they walk that wire, otherwise they will fall. Balance is crucial in every aspect of our lives, whatever it may be.

In God's plan and creation, things are made to balance out. When we look at life, whether we are Christians or non-Christians, in ministry or otherwise, we need to have balance as our anchor, cultivating it daily into our thoughts and actions.

Where do we find such a balance? We find it in the Word of God. The Bible presents us with that proper, whole and complete understanding —a stable approach of thought and action. All truth has two sides, just as a bird flies with two wings. Have you ever seen a bird with one wing fly? If you have ever seen one, I guarantee you it did not fly for long. The bird has been given two wings so that it can soar away from the earth and experience the awesomeness of God's creation and majesty, appreciating the vastness of God's handiwork. We also are meant to soar in this life. But like the bird, we cannot fly with just one wing, no matter how strong and healthy that one wing may be. With only one wing, we are unable to stay aflight due to unbalanced thinking, behaviors and decisions. If we focus only on one side of the coin, we do not have the whole picture and are therefore incomplete.

We must be especially careful of this imbalance when it comes to living a life that is radical for Christ. Many times people are drawn to certain movements or ministries because they operate on the radical edge—that craziness and foolishness for Christ's sake. This type of commitment often brings a breath of fresh air in a place where ministries become dull after time. That edge is good, yet we should keep that edge without becoming too extreme. Maintaining a balance is critical to the health of any individual or organization.

If you look at many movements, you will find that radical edge—in the early days, that is. Unfortunately, many become watered-down over time. Thinking they have been too radical, full of zeal, working day and night, many feel the need to become "normal." And normal often means lukewarm, becoming like everybody else, operating according to the standards of the world. This results in the loss of passion and purpose. Now all that remains is a structure and shadow—an organizational framework.

We should personally seek to live lives of continual commitment and abandonment—forsaking all and following the Lord. We must continually endeavor to keep that vision alive. We do not want to become lukewarm. However, unless we are careful, our desire to be alive and impassioned can produce an unbalanced extreme.

We are living in a day when extremism is clearly evident, especially when it comes to religious matters. Many cults started with Bible studies and good intentions. They did not begin as cults, but became one as they fell out of balance.

When I first visited the United States, I read a shocking article in a newspaper about a group of people in Louisiana. The members of this group were picking up venomous snakes and drinking the poison, declaring that God would keep them safe from the harmful affects. Many of these people died while proving their "faith." Then there is the story about parents in certain churches letting their children die from diseases, keeping them from medical treatment and claiming "faith."

One family, after praying for their diabetic son, threw away his insulin. The poor child died. It was all in the name of "faith"—an extreme and unbalanced faith.

Please let us beware. Satan is the master deceiver. He masquerades as an angel of light. He will seek to sidetrack us with religious thinking that is unbalanced. The more intense and radical our lives are in following the Lord, the more authentic and holy we want to be in our pursuit of God, then the more we are in danger of getting out of balance and going to extremes.

One reason why there has been so much division, disunity and fighting in the Body of Christ throughout history is because an individual or group took a truth, stretched it to an extreme and left out the other side of the story. They forgot that the coin always has two sides and that the bird flies with two wings.

For example, take the Calvinistic and the Armenian points of view. The Calvinists believe in predestination, the election of the saints. Man has nothing to do with it; God has already chosen those who will go to heaven. The Armenians believe in the free will of man to choose. So it is up to man to decide if he is going to heaven or hell by his own choice to receive or reject Christ. These two groups never seem to come to terms. Yet both positions are taught in Scripture. It is like two sides of the *same* coin.

I've had my own personal experience with this. At one time, somebody heard a few of my talks that I gave for the staff and some of the teaching that I did for the Seminary in India. Afterwards this person came to me and said, "I am so confused about your teaching. I heard several of your messages. They all contradict each other. One message is totally one way on a subject and the next time it's the opposite way on the same subject. There doesn't seem to be any cohesion."

Gently I tried to explain to this person, "It's alright. Please understand that when I speak in a meeting there is time for only part of the story. Even after two or three times of speaking, there still may not be enough time to bring the full balance to a particular subject." I feel badly many times because people often do not realize there is always the other side of the story in the messages I speak. If I have five or six opportunities to speak on a certain issue, then I can bring balance. Unfortunately, someone who reads only one book I have written or hears me speak just one time might think that I am completely one-sided. But then they hear me in some other situation and realize my position is not at all what they thought it to be at first.

Sometimes the Bible appears to contradict itself, but actually through these types of Scriptures we find the balance God desires. For example, Jesus said, "But when you do a charitable deed, do not let your left hand know what your right hand is doing, that your charitable deed may be in secret; and your Father who sees in secret will Himself reward you openly" (Matthew 6:3–4). But, on the other hand, He said, "Live such good lives among the pagans that, though they accuse you of doing wrong, they may see your good deeds and glorify God on the day he visits us" (1 Peter 2:12, NIV). There is both the life beneath the soil and the life above the soil. There is that balance.

Proverbs 30:8–9 says, "Give me neither poverty nor riches—feed me with the food allotted to me; lest I be full and deny You, and say, 'Who is the LORD?' Or lest I be poor and steal, and profane the name of my God." It is not being rich or being poor that is important. What is important is honoring God.

James talks about rich people—the millionaires of today—coming to church wearing gold rings and fine clothes. But the point James is trying to get across has nothing to do with rich people selling all their gold and expensive things. Instead, he says not to give more honor to the rich people than to the poor people who come (see James 2:3–4). You see, in the church you have both groups—rich and poor. The balance is kept with love, not with external agendas.

Another example of how things can get out of balance can be seen in the life of Martin

Luther. The Reformation started based on the teaching of faith—that our salvation is by faith in Jesus Christ, not by works. "The righteous will live by faith" (Romans 1:17, NIV). "Without faith it is impossible to please God" (Hebrews 11:6, NIV). This was a great revelation to Luther because his church at that time was preaching a salvation based on works and good deeds.

But when Martin Luther read James, he saw that it talked also about works. "What use is it, my brethren, if someone says he has faith but he has no works? Can that faith save him? . . . Even so faith, if it has no works, is dead, being by itself" (James 2:14, 17, NASB). Luther could not grasp this. He grappled with the message of the book of James to such a degree that he didn't think it should be part of the Bible. He had come out of the works position into the faith position, and he could not see the whole picture.

In reality, there is a beautiful balance between faith and works. We can see a picture of it in the life of Abraham. Around the age of 75, Abraham was promised a son. Twenty-five years later at the age of 100, his body was "as good as dead," and his wife's was also (see Romans 4). Physically, they were too old to have children. So how did Abraham and Sarah get their son? It was not a virgin birth. Abraham had a part to play. God used his body, his energy, and his blood to bring forth a son. Abraham could have said, "God promised, so He'll do it," and just sat there. But he didn't do that. That's what it means when it says faith without works is dead. When Abraham offered his son Isaac, it was a real offering up—a work. He took Isaac in his own hands, laid him on the altar and raised the knife. Real faith has action; it is visible; it is a faith with works.

Over and over again we see this balance in the Scriptures. God's throne is built on the foundation of mercy and justice. It is not built on mercy alone or justice alone. There is balance. He is the God of Jacob, who was a crook, a deceiver and a liar. Yet He is also the God of Israel, which means "prince of God."

There is both work and rest. The two are not incompatible. In fact, Jesus speaks of the two existing simultaneously. "Take My yoke upon you and learn from Me, for I am gentle and lowly in heart, and you will find rest for your souls. For My yoke is easy and My burden is light" (Matthew 11:29-30).

In all of our maturing and growing in understanding and living as the Body of Christ, we need to be continually called back to balanced thinking. And that proper balance is given to us through the Word of God.

CHAPTER TWO

Our Need and Christ's Sufficiency

We all have expectations for ourselves. We all have ways we would like to be different. Perhaps we would like to be more patient or less prone to anger. When we do not measure up to the standards we have set for ourselves we become discouraged. But we have to realize that God is not discouraged with us. He never gives up on us. He never stops working with us. Balance is needed between knowing our sins and insufficiency and knowing that it is God who works within us, perfecting us for His glory.

When you pray, do you oftentimes get weighed down with confessing your own sins and repenting for every wrong thought and failure? Sometimes it seems we can't get over this, living with constant memories from the past and old sins that caused great pain. Many people live continually with the words, "If only . . . if only . . . I wish," playing through their minds, unable to move past their failures.

Sometimes we feel that we don't pray enough. We are not spiritual enough. We don't have enough of a burden for the lost. We feel we are not good husbands, good fathers, good wives, good mothers or good children. We think negative things about ourselves, and we begin to dwell on these thoughts, beating ourselves up because we don't spend money wisely, don't study enough or don't pray enough.

We all have this problem—me included. Our expectations of ourselves can take us into spiritual darkness. This happens because we become our own judge. We become our law. We become our guide and teacher, the one who evaluates ourself. In the end, it is a cesspool of self-centeredness and anguish.

Matthew 12:20 says, "A bruised reed He will not break, and smoking flax He will not quench." Philippians 1:6 says, "He who has begun a good work in you will complete it until the day of Jesus Christ." Philippians 2:13 says, "For it is God who works in you both to will and to do for His good pleasure."

Ten looks at self and one look at Jesus will make you a hypocrite. You will have to pretend to be spiritual, living with conflict and mental torture because you don't measure up to your own standards. Hear the frustration in Paul's voice when he writes of the great insufficiency of *I* in Romans 7:14–23. If you are this kind of individual there is no rest for you. This happens because you become too introspective, taking the focus off of Christ and placing it on yourself.

But one look at self and ten looks at Jesus will keep you going. Romans 7:24–25 says, "O wretched man that I am! Who will deliver me from this body of death? I thank God— through Jesus Christ our Lord!" Yes! It is through Jesus Christ our Lord!

It is good to know our weaknesses and failures, for how can we confess our sins unless we see them as sins? Toward the end of his life, Paul calls himself the worst of sinners (see 1 Timothy 1:15), knowing that in his flesh there dwelt nothing that was good. This is being honest about our true condition. But in this honesty, we must also know God's longsuffering and faithfulness in working with us in our many weaknesses.

It is in knowing our true condition that we understand the fullness and completeness of God's great love for us. We could never fully understand and appreciate what Christ has done for us until we know something of our wretched state. Knowing the offense in us causes us to understand the depth of His grace—that while we were yet sinners, Christ died for us. The danger lies in *dwelling* on our sins, failures and shortcomings.

We must look to Christ, the author and finisher of our faith, the giver of all good gifts—our Master, Savior, Redeemer and Friend. We must trust Him. We must have faith that He will mold us into His image and that He will not give up on us. It took 20 years for God to make Jacob into Israel. But did God give up on him? No.

High standards are very good. We encourage people to read *The Road to Reality,*[1] *The Calvary Road,*[2] *True Discipleship*[3] and other books whose authors challenge a deeper life and commitment. The tremendous challenge is to constantly abandon all and follow the Lord—walking away from friendship with the world and keeping ourselves free from the pollution of watered-down Christianity.

None of us is capable of serving God in our own strength. That is good. None of us measures up. It is the strength and grace of Jesus that allows us to serve. "With men this is impossible, but with God all things are possible" (Matthew 19:26). We have to fully understand both parts of this verse—the first part, "with man this is impossible" and the second part, "but *with God* all things are possible" (emphasis added).

Keep in mind—wherever you are in your spiritual walk with the Lord, God is not concerned about whether you are now a mature, strong person. No. He is looking at your heart. Let Him work with you. Trust Him to do His work in you.

I want to encourage you. When you have these struggles in your spiritual life—when you feel weak, like you are not measuring up—just be yourself. Admit your sins and shortcomings. Don't try to prove anything to anyone. The worst thing you can do is become a hypocrite and pretender. One thing God hates more than anything else is hypocrisy.

Let us be honest with each other. I share my weaknesses and problems. One time when I was speaking to seminary students, I shared about the struggles I have in many areas of my life. It shocked the students. One of them said to me afterwards, "We never thought someone like you would have struggles in your life."

I replied, "You must be joking!" The truth is we all struggle with one thing or another. But even when you are discouraged about yourself, God is not. He loves you. He has forgiven your sins—the ones you have committed, the ones you are committing and the ones you will commit until the last second of your life. It's all taken care of.

You cannot make yourself spiritual by weeping and fasting and punishing yourself. As much as you are concerned about your inner life, putting yourself down and dwelling on failures and sins will not help. Remember, it is God who is working with you and He will not let you go. He is faithful to complete the good work He started in you.

CHAPTER THREE

Our Sacrifice and God's Grace

In the four Gospels, Jesus talks about forsaking all, giving up everything, not laying up treasures on earth and being willing to walk away from even your own life. First Corinthians 13:3 says, "And though I bestow all my goods to feed the poor, and though I give my body to be burned, but have not love, it profits me nothing." Unless the motivation behind the sacrifices we make is love—unselfish and genuinely motivated by God and His grace—our sacrifice profits nothing.

The teachings laid out in books such as *True Discipleship*[1] need to be balanced by those presented in books such as *Grace Awakening*.[2] The church at Ephesus made great sacrifices,

A Life of Balance

worked hard and endured difficult times. But the Lord said to them, "Nevertheless I have this against you, that you have left your first love. Remember therefore from where you have fallen; repent and do the first works, or else I will come to you quickly and remove your lampstand from its place—unless you repent" (Revelation 2:4–5). He said this simply because they had lost the reason for all the sacrifice and work; they had lost their first love—Jesus.

One of the marks of people who serve God with great sacrifice, but without the inner reality of grace and love, is that they criticize and condemn others, putting them down and finding fault. They look at others' houses and think something is wrong with them for living in such wealth or squalor. They look at their clothes. They look at their kids. They compare and complain and murmur, despising people who may not even have the so-called "deeper life," or revelations and gifts of the Holy Spirit that they have.

The older son in Luke 15 was much like this. While the younger brother was squandering the father's wealth with wild living, he was laboring in the field as a full-time worker, sweating away. He was not wasting his father's money. But he was full of jealousy, anger and bitterness. He had a condemning and unloving spirit. He imagined that his younger brother had done all sorts of wicked sins, such as living with prostitutes, all of which the younger brother may have actually never done. He accused his father. I can imagine him saying, "How can you claim that you are my father and that you love me? I've been with you all these years, and you haven't ever given me a party. Yet my wicked brother returns, and look what you do for him."

This attitude is the fruit of legalism and Phariseeism. It is sacrifice combined with a hard, unloving heart, and it is no good. That is why it is so important to keep a balance between living a life of sacrifice and extending grace and love to all.

I will not change the message I gave you in *The Road to Reality*[3] about sacrificing comforts and giving up worldly possessions for God's eternal work. I will not compromise, because I keep telling myself that 100 years from now, earthly possessions aren't going to matter. But I regret those days when I spoke that message without grace.

One particular time comes to mind. I was invited to a home in the Midwestern United States to speak to a group of medical doctors about missions. This house was like the Taj Mahal or some great palace. I sat there fuming, angry and upset at the wealth I saw. I said to myself, "These peoples lives are all a show. Why can't they sell all this and give the money to world missions?" I could hardly wait for the chance to speak. When my time came to speak, I said nothing about the fancy house. But what I did say was so harsh, unkind and judgmental. My attitude was so unlike Christ.

God in His mercy helped me to grow up and understand His heart. Then I learned there are millionaires who love God and serve Him with more commitment than many full-time Christian workers I know.

In Philippians 4:11–12 Paul writes, "I have learned to be content whatever the circum-stances. I know what it is to be in need, and I know what it is to have plenty. I have learned the secret of being content in any and every situation, whether well fed or hungry, whether living in plenty or in want" (NIV). We must learn to live with this attitude. Simply put, Paul is saying, "If you put me in a five-star hotel, I am very happy. Bring all the best food, the caviar. And if you put me in a no-star hotel, no problem. I am content and happy there, too."

If you are called by the Lord to be a person of sacrifice, if you are given the grace to give things up, I can tell you, it is wonderful. I could not have given up the things I held on to if it were not for the grace and the love of God. As the Lord is my witness, I found such joy and love in giving them up. I never felt sadness and sorrow in surrendering these things. Instead I got such joy—joy that nothing in the world could give me. It was God's grace.

We cannot impose His calling for us on others or assume that others are wrong or less mature because they do things differently. It is the Lord's work in us, not our own doing, that makes us willing and happy to surrender these things.

CHAPTER FOUR

The Devil Is Bad Enough

It is so important that we strive to maintain a balance between attributing things to demonic activity and recognizing natural phenomena. A particular instance comes to mind when I think of this subject. It was a time many years ago when I was speaking at a church. After the meeting a lady came up to me and said, "Brother K.P., will you please lay your hand on me and pray for me?" Naturally, I asked what she wanted me to pray for.

She answered, "I have a demon of smoking."

I replied, "Dear lady, you don't have a demon. You can cast out demons, but you cannot cast out the flesh."

For every flare of temper, every weakness,

every time you sneeze, you may think, "Oh, there is a demon." Your car just swerved into the next lane or some madman drove through the red light. "Oh, there's a demon attacking me." No. The Devil is bad enough. Don't attribute every little bad thing that happens to him.

Please don't look at the events in your life and think demons are after you all the time. There *are* demons and there *are* attacks. But we should be careful not to become paranoid of the things that happen in life. If there are demons, the Lord has given us the authority to pray and tell them to leave—and they must go.

The truth is, the Devil is defeated. Therefore, the child of God has no reason to be afraid of Satan and his hordes of demons. Someone who has truly repented of sin and trusts in the Lord Jesus Christ lives a life that has been washed in the blood of the Lamb. When Jesus died on the cross, He placed demons and Satan—the whole evil bunch— under His feet. And we are the Body of Christ, so the whole satanic force is under our feet. The Scripture specifically tells us, "Greater is He who is in you than he who is in the world" (1 John 4:4, NASB).

One of the main tactics that Satan uses is causing us to forget who we are in Christ. This deception is very powerful. When we forget that Satan was defeated through the death of the Lord Jesus Christ on the cross, we also forget the greatness of our God. In Ephesians 1:20–23, we read of the tremendous authority that the Lord Jesus Christ has given to His Body, that is, each one of us who belongs to the Lord:

> . . . when He raised Him from the dead and seated Him at His right hand in the heavenly places, far above all principality and power and might and dominion, and every name that is named, not only in this age but also in that which is to come. And He put all things under His feet, and gave Him to be head over all things to the church, which is His body, the fullness of Him who fills all in all.

For many of us, we constantly see the Enemy and his tactics all around, and we focus on what we see rather than on the power of our God. This is clearly illustrated in the story of the 12 spies who were sent out to evaluate the Promised Land (see Numbers 13). Except for Joshua and Caleb, 10 of them—the majority—came back talking about the giants they saw in the land and how they could never conquer them. It even says in Numbers 13:33, "There we saw the giants . . . and we were like grasshoppers in our own sight, and so we were in their sight." They made the confession that it was impossible to possess the land God had promised them. The problem was not the giants—it was that they saw *only* the giants. What they overlooked was the greatness of God in the situation and how God saw them—able to possess the land by His might!

This is so true in our lives today as well. When dealing with daily life struggles and issues, especially if they are influenced by satanic forces, we can easily forget that God is just that—God! Ephesians 6:16 (NASB) tells us we should take up "the shield of faith with which you will be able to extinguish all the flaming arrows of the evil one." That means no matter what we face, we are given the authority, and we can overcome and stand firm and victorious.

At the same time, we need to be very careful that we do not look at people with emotional problems or certain mental problems as being demon possessed. Just like there are large numbers of people living with physical illness, there are thousands and tens of thousands of people who are inflicted with some form of emotional or mental problem. What they need is counseling based on God's Word and treatment by professional people.

Please understand. There are very real physical and mental illnesses. With some of these you can pray against demons all you want, but that is not going to work. These people need treatment, help and counseling. At the same time, some people *are* demonized, as seen in Mark 5:1–20. Nothing will help them except praying and casting out the demon.

There are natural phenomenas, calamities, problems and difficulties in life. But there is also demonic activity that needs to be recognized for what it is. Unless we are careful, we can get out of balance and forget there are two sides.

CHAPTER FIVE

Faith and Common Sense

Nothing is going to be accomplished for eternity without faith. Only that which is done by faith will last. It is impossible to please God without faith (see Hebrews 11:6). Faith is the foundation of everything. Salvation will never happen without faith. Sanctification will never happen without faith. Heaven will never be ours without faith. But we need to be careful not to embrace foolish steps of ungrounded "faith." We need to keep a balance between faith and the common sense God has given us.

The ministry of Gospel for Asia is a testimony to the power of faith in action. The Lord has done so many incredible things that we alone could have never made happen. What God promised to do, He will do. Faith is one of the subjects I like to talk about, because I see it working continually.

Oftentimes, people forget that we cannot respond beyond the measure of faith we have received from the Lord. When we hear incredible stories of God's dealings with other people, surely it encourages our hearts to believe God for greater things. But in all of this, we must guard against the tendency to exercise "faith" not in line with God's purposes. We cannot decide on something "good" we want to have happen and then presume God will do it if we keep on praying. We must not fall into the "name-it-and-claim-it" trap. God's definition of "good" is so much greater than ours. He has our spiritual well-being in His perspective. For a lot of people in Christendom, faith has become a magic wand that will do wonders to meet certain wishes and wants. This type of "faith" is totally self-centered, leaving no room for God's glory or the extension of the Lord's kingdom in someone's life. Hebrews 11 shows those whom God considered people of faith; their lives were spent continually for the glory of God, and they paid the price with their life.

When we read about David facing the giant Goliath and defeating him, and Abraham getting a son even though his natural body was incapable of producing such, and the wall of Jericho falling down, and about all the many incredible miracles recorded in the Gospels—the blind man seeing and the leper healed—we stand amazed to see how these individuals believed God and held onto His promises.

We need to realize that the faith they had was not something they could cook up. Rather, it was based on what they heard and learned about the grace and the promises of the living God. We, too, are given the challenge and encouragement to believe and have faith for God to do wonders on our behalf.

Let us be careful not to presume on God and take foolish steps, acting out of presumption. I pray for sick people often, and I see God heal and do miracles. I have seen people recover from illnesses for which there was no treatment. But does that mean I don't take medicine? No.

I have a friend who is a well-known preacher, whom God used to do outstanding miracles. I was an eyewitness to what happened. The blind saw. Totally deaf people heard, and mute people spoke. I was right there when these things happened. One day this pastor told me that he had developed a heart problem. Up to that point, he had experienced continual healing in his life, and he was scared to go to a doctor. But the Lord spoke to his heart and said, "If you don't go to a doctor, you are going to die. If you go to a doctor and get treatment, you will live." So he went to the hospital, had surgery and lived.

I asked him why he thought this had happened. He told me that he believed the Lord wanted to show him that He heals through medicine and doctors. God wanted him to help other people see this, too, so that they were not led into blind faith. It is not God's intent that people die because they refuse medical attention. My friend realized that the whole experience was God's plan to help him understand the balance needed in this area.

God is the author and finisher of our faith. Faith is something He gives us through His Word and in proportion to our readiness to receive it. We cannot generate our own faith through the flesh and positive thinking. We need to have understanding so we can discern these things. It is absolutely essential to keep a balance between faith and common sense so that we do not fall into counterfeit faith.

CHAPTER SIX

Authority and Submission

This is a subject with incredible, potential problems and difficulties. The Bible teaches very strongly about obeying authorities over us. The entire kingdom of God is meant to function in an orderly manner under God's plan of authority. But there is an extreme teaching on submission to leaders in authority, wives to husbands, children to parents, and political or religious leaders to others that can be dangerous, unless we balance it with the fact that each individual must know that he is also responsible to God, His law and His Word. The balance must be kept between submission and individual guidance.

Romans 13:1–2 (NIV) says, "Everyone must submit himself to the governing authorities, for there is no authority except that which God has established. The authorities that exist have been established by God. Consequently, he who rebels against authority is rebelling against what God has instituted." First Thessalonians 5:12 (NIV) says, "Now we ask you, brothers, to respect those who work hard among you, who are over you in the Lord and who admonish you." Clearly God's plan is that we live in submission to God-given authority. Watchman Nee, in his book *Spiritual Authority*[1], specifically states that in Scripture, rebellion, either passive or active, is sin.

Pay attention. Lucifer *became* a devil. He was not created a devil. In fact, he began as the most amazing, beautiful archangel, the highest of all angels created by God. But he became the devil as a result of rebellion and insubordination. His pride led him to step out from under God's authority and set himself up as ruler.

Korah destroyed himself and many others by not following God's plan of authority and recognizing Moses as God's leader (see Numbers 16). Saul sinned by not waiting for Samuel, the prophet with God-given authority, to conduct the sacrifice (see 1 Samuel 13). Gehazi did not follow the leading of his master, Elisha. He accepted gifts for the healing of Naaman's leprosy and, as a consequence, became a leper himself (see 2 Kings 5). God's order in the family is for the husband to be the leader, for the wife to submit and follow him, and for the children to follow the parents. The Bible is filled with this teaching (see Ephesians 5–6).

But in this teaching there also needs to be balance. Look at the lives of Daniel and Esther. Each had to stand for God in a situation in which there were leaders in authority over them. Daniel was thrown to the lions for his refusal to obey the king's decree. Esther had to approach the king uninvited, an action that could have led to her death, in order to plead for her people.

Tens of thousands of lives have been destroyed through false teaching and extremism about submission. Some leaders can become unbalanced. I am not just talking about cults. In some congregations, there is a sort of "shepherding theology." Under its teaching, people are told that they must consult their elders concerning what type of clothes they should wear, what house they should buy and where they should work. In the end, these people stop thinking for themselves and going to God for direction. Instead, they become like slaves, following the ideas of their leader rather than God, and their lives are destroyed.

Look at Jesus, Paul, Peter and others in the New Testament. Not once did these men force anyone to submit to anything. They gave guidelines for holy living. They spelled out principles and lived by them. They preached and taught freedom—freedom from traditions, freedom from sin and freedom to live a godly life. They did not seek to control behaviors or thoughts. Submission is a choice people make to follow the Lord as their leaders follow the Lord.

One of my regrets in this area of submission is how I acted toward my wife during the first two years of our married life. I was not sensitive to her at all. I was determined that I was going to be the leader and that she must obey everything. When something went wrong, she was the one to ask for forgiveness. I didn't ask for forgiveness, of course, because I was the husband. That is what I saw when I was growing up, and that is how I thought things should be.

Things went on like this for a couple of years. Then God heard Gisela's prayers and opened my eyes, causing me to realize that she was not my slave. From then on, things changed. I began to think about my wife as a human being, considering her needs, emotions and feelings. I learned practical things, like how to change diapers, cook, wash clothes and clean house. These were not part of my household when I grew up. They were things I had never done before. But God was teaching me that being in authority is about being a servant. I became quick to repent and ask forgiveness when I was wrong. I realized I must care for Gisela and love her, like Christ loved the Church and cared for her. I must not misuse her. I must not take advantage of her. I must not order her around and control her, but love her. Love does not force people to do things a particular way.

In any movement, any group, in each home—everywhere—God places leaders. But please understand: Jesus said, "Whoever wants to become great among you must be your servant, and whoever wants to be first must be slave of all. For even the Son of Man did not come to be served but to serve" (Mark 10:43–45, NIV). Jesus led by example. We also must lead others through love, patience and example. We lead others through bearing with them in their suffering, not through beating them into obedience.

CHAPTER SEVEN

Discipline and Freedom

Setting good habits for ourselves and be-ing disciplined in our lives are good. But it is not good to become a slave to that sort of disciplined life. The Pharisees were very disciplined people. They fasted. They prayed regularly. They studied the Scriptures. And they were also bound by their traditions and discipline. The same thing can happen to us Christians today. "It is for freedom that Christ has set us free" (Galatians 5:1, NIV). There needs to be a balance between discipline and freedom.

Some of the unhappiest people I have ever met in my life are those who are militant about everything in their lives. They must always have things together, always be on time, perfect in every way. These perfectionists make their own lives miserable, as well as everyone else with whom they come in contact. These people are controlled, not by grace and freedom, but by legalism.

Someone once said, "Nothing will keep a Christian more immature than trying to keep a list." Having a disciplined life is important—very important—especially in the areas of personal discipline (such as prayer life, time management, systematic study of the Bible). Yet some people become so paranoid about doing all these things with a legalistic mindset that they actually become slaves of these disciplines. They first embraced them because they believed the discipline would bring freedom to their lives. But now they are enslaved by them, and their daily life is one big burden of endless striving. And it doesn't end with themselves either. People who live like this will often use their own standards to judge others. They constantly become critical and judgmental toward their spouses, children and fellow workers. These kinds of people are absolutely miserable to live with.

In his book *He Still Moves Stones*, Max Lucado states, "Legalism: Turns my opinion into your burden. . . . Turns my opinion into your boundary. . . . Turns my opinion into your obligation."[1] There needs to be a balance in the way we handle our own life of discipline and how we respond to others. In Romans 14 we find the instruction about giving freedom and grace *to others*—living by the law of love, not of discipline. When we become judgmental and critical toward the people around us, we make their lives hard and difficult. Romans 14:13 says, "Therefore let us not judge one another anymore, but rather resolve this, not to put a stumbling block or a cause to fall in our brother's way." It is good to have a disciplined life and make personal demands on ourselves. But at the same time, we must show grace and mercy toward others who may not be like us or who disagree with us, and bear with one another in love and humility.

In Romans 7, Paul talks about the incredible struggle in his own life to find victory and peace through "rigid discipline." These demands only made him more miserable and wretched as he kept striving to be perfect. The truth of the matter is this: Although we must do our part, we also must realize that if our part is all there is, then everything begins with us and ends with us. And the Scripture says, "Nothing good dwells in me" (Romans 7:18, NASB).

Toward the end of Romans 7, we hear Paul bursting out with joy and celebration because he realized there is true freedom and victory—not in rigid discipline, but in *yielding all that he was to Christ* who came to set him free. Romans 7:24–25 says, "O wretched man that I am! Who will deliver me from this body of death? I thank God—through Jesus Christ our Lord!"

My encouragement to you is this: Be disciplined, absolutely. You must be. Yet don't let that become your master and your god. Don't become militant about organizing your every minute. Don't try so hard to save time that you forget to live. Don't become so scheduled that you demand from yourself and everybody else a perfectly structured life. There is no joy, no freedom, in that kind of living. Ask God to order your time. If you are in the middle of a scheduled prayer time and someone knocks on the door, don't automatically ignore the knock. Ask God. Maybe He has sent this person to pray for you or maybe this person needs your comfort. Don't be undisciplined, but at the same time rest in the assurance that "the steps of a good man are ordered by the LORD" (Psalm 37:23).

CHAPTER EIGHT

Where Is Your Focus?

A balance needs to be kept between our concerns for a deeper life and our concerns for world evangelism. God wants us to grow and become more like Him. He wants us to know Him intimately. He is a jealous God who longs for our fellowship and seeks our undivided love and attention. All this is true. But it is also true that He has sent us into the world as His representatives to seek the lost. Jesus said, "Go into all the world and preach the gospel to every creature" (Mark 16:15).

It is good to desire a deeper life, and it is good to go forth telling of Jesus. But we will only have a balance in these things when our focus is on Christ and Christ alone. Paul had a desire to know God and a desire to preach the Good News. Both desires existed simultaneously because both are in God's heart. The same should be true of us.

I encourage you to go to the average Christian bookstore sometime and look at the titles spread all over the shelves. The majority of them are about how to fix your life or how to get a deeper life. But how many books are there about half of the world going to hell? How many books do you see talking about the needs of millions in unreached areas?

The other extreme is being people who are so full of zeal, constantly driven by the great need around them. We cannot work in the flesh and have no understanding of the Lord in our inner life. We must be people who continually seek the face of God to know Him.

There must be a harmony in developing our intimate walk with the Lord and our passion to reach the lost. If I really know Jesus who gave His life on the cross and shed His blood to save sinners, how can I not want to save people? How can I say that I know Jesus, or how can I enjoy a life of deeply loving Jesus, and not be compelled to do whatever I can to reach the lost world? We should not become unbalanced by all the deeper life teaching that we forget the reality of the lost world.

Anything of a truly deeper life culminates with us becoming more like Christ—having the mind of Christ. And Christ died for the world and paid the price for us to be saved and to spread this Good News to everyone. If we keep our focus on *Christ*—not specifically on gaining a deeper life for ourselves or on reaching the millions—there will be this balance.

CHAPTER NINE

Zeal with Wisdom

When you read about Paul, Peter, Philip and others in the book of Acts, you see how their lives were marked by passion. They were full of zeal, enthusiasm and excitement, red-hot in following the Lord. Nothing could stop them.

I believe the Lord desires for us to be the same way today. Even Jesus had a direct purpose and a goal. He pressed onward toward Jerusalem with an iron will, focused on what His Father required of Him. And so must we—but not at the expense of wisdom. As somebody once said, "We can become so heavenly minded that we are of no earthly good." We need to be wise in our zeal. Sometimes we need to slow down, be sensitive and listen. In all His zeal, Jesus still took time to simply listen to the woman at the well and play with the children.

One time when I came home from the office, Gisela was crying about something going on at the house. I don't remember exactly what it was that was bothering her. I automatically started quoting Bible verses and preaching to her, thinking that was what she needed to hear. She stopped me in mid-sentence, saying, "Can you please stop? I can preach all those sermons and quote all those Bible verses too. I just want you to listen." In my enthusiasm and zeal, I had completely missed what she needed. There was no wisdom in that.

There are many different ways that zeal without wisdom can manifest. Numerous times, women have come to me asking for prayer for their unsaved husband. They explain the strife and incredible pain they live with, telling me all the ways they have tried to convert their loved one, but to no avail. Often, this zeal takes a turn, and soon the wife starts criticizing, putting down and pointing out all the husband's wrong ways. In turn, the husband is driven even further from the Gospel than he was before. And further from his wife.

Zeal to see a loved one come to know the Lord is good. The Bible shows us the wise way to handle this zeal—and it never mentions to argue and fight or tell the whole world how bad someone may be. Rather, in meekness and gentleness, we are to live a godly life before that person. This becomes the means for someone to come to know the Lord (see 1 Peter 3:1–7).

How often we end up losing precious friends and bringing such disunity in our fellowship or in our home by handling the truth without wisdom.

Once a pastor came to visit the GFA office. As I spent time with him, he began telling me all the things he was doing for mission work. Something within me wanted to rise up and say, "This guy is off-the-wall. He is so completely ignorant about what is really going on." I wanted to explain the whole picture to him and give him the real story of world missions. But suddenly I thought to myself, "There is a time for everything. Is this the time to do it? He is so happy, so enthusiastic. He wants to pour out his heart and tell me what all he has done and where all he has gone. If I start lecturing at him now, what would be the point? I must love him and respect him and honor him. Dignity should be given to him."

So I listened . . . and listened . . . and listened. I said, "Wonderful, I am so glad you have been to this place." And then I said, "May I have your business card so I can contact you again?" Then I gave him my book *Revolution in World Missions*[1] and said, "When you have finished reading it, would you give me a call?" He said he would.

Ten years ago, I would have acted differently. I would have said, "You think you know this and that! Well, let me tell you, you are wrong. It's really like this . . . " But this is not how the Lord would have responded. We need to make a conscious effort to be sensitive to one another in this way. We need to keep our zeal and walk in wisdom at the same time.

Wisdom is knowing how to properly handle the information and knowledge we have, especially when it comes to relationships. And the Word of God tells us we receive wisdom by having the fear of the Lord. That simply means a close relationship with the Lord, seeking His face and living in obedience. This brings wisdom to our hearts.

CHAPTER TEN

Love and Doctrine

The balance between sound doctrine and love is imperative. Doctrine is important, and the Word will always be our final authority, keeping us on course; but love must always remain our means of travel.

There are those who say that all we have to be concerned about is full-fledged ecumenism among all churches and denominations, regardless of what they believe or do not believe. Keep in mind, however, that the apostle Paul spent half of his life defending the faith that he preached because of the apostasy that began to creep in and destroy so many churches. As you read the writings of Paul, you will see that he was a man aching with such a burden for the purity of the faith and the truth of the Word of God.

Church history clearly shows that when the Word of God is not taught and commitment to doctrinal purity is not maintained, the Church enters into a dark age. Examples of this are found throughout the centuries. Had it not been for Martin Luther, who in the sixteenth century stood up to defend the purity of doctrines, risking his very own life, the Church might have remained in utter darkness. The Reformation, which was the fruit of his life, took place because of the preaching and defending of God's Word.

Even today, all over the world, the Church at large is once again moving toward another dark period due to the liberalism being taught and perpetuated in great numbers in many theological institutions. Not giving heed to sound doctrine will lead to syncretism and pluralism. And these have become some of the most serious, destructive forces throughout the church today.

Paul warned Timothy to take care of the sound doctrine he received, while at the same time continuing in the grace and love of Christ. In his letters to Timothy we read Paul's exhortations concerning this balance: "Hold fast the pattern of sound words which you have heard from me, in faith and love

which are in Christ Jesus" (2 Timothy 1:13).
"O Timothy! Guard what was committed to
your trust, avoiding the profane and idle bab-
blings and contradictions of what is falsely
called knowledge—by professing it some
have strayed concerning the faith" (1 Timothy 6:20–21). "Be strong in the grace that is
in Christ Jesus. And the things that you have
heard from me among many witnesses, commit these to faithful men who will be able to
teach others also" (2 Timothy 2:1–2).

Another example of this balance to be
kept is found in Revelation 2:2–5, a passage in
which Christ speaks to the church at Ephesus.
These believers had pure doctrine and were
extremely fundamental in their faith. Yet the
Lord said that He would put out their light
because of their lack of love.

Love must be the root and foundation of
all that we do in our service for the Lord. Let
us not forget the exhortation in 1 Corinthians 13—"Though I speak with the tongues of
men and of angels, but have not love, I have
become sounding brass or a clanging cymbal.
And though I have the gift of prophecy, and
understand all mysteries and all knowledge,
and though I have all faith, so that I could
remove mountains, but have not love, I am
nothing. And though I bestow all my goods
to feed the poor, and though I give my body

to be burned, but have not love, it profits me nothing. Love never fails. But whether there are prophecies, they will fail; whether there are tongues, they will cease; whether there is knowledge, it will vanish away. Now abide faith, hope, love, these three; but the *greatest of these is love*" (1 Corinthians 13:1–3, 8, 13, emphasis added). Without love, all means nothing.

The Church is called to evangelize the world and to call all men to become part of the Body of Christ. But this purpose can only be carried out as we walk in love. In John 13:34–35, Jesus said to His disciples, "A new command I give you: Love one another. As I have loved you, so you must love one another. By this all men will know that you are my disciples, if you love one another" (NIV). In his classic book *Love Covers*,[1] Paul Billheimer says the biggest hindrance for the world to come to know the Lord Jesus Christ is the sin of unloving attitudes and division in the Body of Christ. I fully agree.

We must be very careful not to make rigid boxes of "our doctrine" and try to squeeze people into them. People have asked me, "Was Mother Teresa a Christian? Is she in heaven?" By some people's denominational teachings, Mother Teresa is not in heaven. Based on what some churches believe today,

many people who headed the Reformation—
bringing enlightenment to the entire Christian
world—will go to hell because they didn't fit
in with "sound" doctrine.

Satan knows that a house divided against
itself cannot stand (see Mark 3:25, NIV). And
so he cunningly seeks to divide the Body of
the Lord Jesus Christ on many minor issues.
Particular subjects that create disunity include
specific views on the Holy Spirit, Calvinism,
Armenians, translations of the Bible, the
second coming of Christ, and many others. I
am convinced that the thousands of divisions
in the Body of Christ today have very little to
do with doctrine. The majority is based on the
overemphasis of minor issues and traditions.
Once we start investigating, it is amazing how
few differences there actually are in fundamental doctrines among most churches. Yet
there is such an unloving attitude and division at large.

Please remember: God is much more
concerned about our heart than our head. I
have met people who are a little "off" in some
doctrines that I consider important. But they
are still people deeply devoted to the Lord,
knowing Him intimately.

How do we explain all this? I am not sure.
I don't have all the answers. But one thing is
certain: The Pharisees, who knew all the an-

swers and had "sound doctrine," are the ones
who crucified Christ. Let us keep in mind that
the most important evidence of those who
follow the Lord Jesus Christ is not seen in
their commitment to fundamental doctrines,
but in their life of love. The world will know
we are Christians by our love, not by our
doctrines. When love is absent, doctrines have
no use. Truth without love is a lie. We must
maintain a balance.

CHAPTER ELEVEN

As You Run to the Finish Line

In the midst of the enormous vision for world evangelization, we need to keep a balance between commitment to our vision and commitment to individuals. We must always see the big picture—like the 2.7 billion unreached people in our generation. But at the same time, we must not lose sight of the individuals the Lord has placed around us. God never forgot the individual. He saw Noah, Abraham, Hannah and David, knowing each by name.

We humans are so easily moved by large numbers and the majority. We see this in the ways of the world—so political that one individual is easily disregarded, sent to the slaughterhouse for the sake of some kind of gain. But God does not operate this way.

In the parable of the lost sheep found in Luke 15, Jesus talked about the importance of one in the midst of a multitude. He spoke of a man with 100 sheep, who, when discovering one little lamb was lost, left the entire fold to search for the one. The shepherd did not say, "Oh well, I've got 99 left. Let the one go. It's okay." No. He left the 99 to pursue the one lost, searching until he found it. Then he carried that one that strayed home on his shoulders, rejoicing. The Lord said, "I tell you that in the same way there will be more rejoicing in heaven over one sinner who repents than over ninety-nine righteous persons who do not need to repent" (Luke 15:7, NIV). The heavens rejoice when just *one* person finds his way to the Father's love.

When I was 16 years old, I was part of a mission organization involving some 450-plus people. Even though I couldn't speak English fluently and was not very qualified, someone saw me as an individual made by God, with potential from Him. If that person had looked only at the entire movement and the big vision God gave, they could have said, "You don't qualify. There's no way to fit you into our system," and passed me by. But somebody was willing to see me, the little individual, in the multitude of people.

The same thing happened in Genesis 16. Here we see the Father's heart for the individual through the story of Hagar, a woman alone and crying out in desperation. Even though Hagar was just an Egyptian maidservant and not a part of the house of Israel, God came down solely to minister to this woman and give her a promise.

Jesus said, "He who has seen Me has seen the Father" (John 14:9). Looking at the way Christ dealt with individuals helps us understand how much He cares about each one of us. Jesus looked for the one man Matthew, a tax collector whom nobody loved or cared for. He sought after one Nicodemus, one Zaccheus, one Samaritan woman, one woman caught in sin, one sick man lying by the pool for 38 years, one blind beggar. This is the nature of the Lord Jesus Christ.

Yet He who spoke to and cared for the individual did not disregard the multitudes. "When [Jesus] saw the multitudes, He was moved with compassion for them, because they were weary and scattered, like sheep having no shepherd" (Matthew 9:36). He cared for millions, while at the same time caring for the individual, finding time even for a handful of little children.

We must see the world, "for God so loved the world" (John 3:16). This verse shows us a glimpse of the Father's love and knowledge, His care and concern for every human being—that means the approximately 6 billion people living on planet Earth at this time in history. At the same time, that statement includes one individual like you and me. In the book of Psalms, the writer says, "As for me, I am poor and needy, but the Lord is thinking about me right now" (Psalm 40:17, NLT).

I heard an amazing incident that took place during the Special Olympics years ago. Nine physically and mentally handicapped children lined up for the 100-meter dash in which the participants trained for months. Finally, the big event was at hand. Everyone readied for the race to begin. At the sound of the gun, they darted off. A few minutes into the race, one boy stumbled, fell to his knees and began to cry.

Sitting there on the track, he looked up to see everyone else running ahead of him to the finish line. Along with the pain in his knees was the pain from everything he had worked so hard for—gone in one fall. The boy's cries filled the track area.

The spectators in the stands heard it, as did the other runners competing. Then the most beautiful thing happened. All the other runners stopped their racing and ran back to the injured boy, helping to lift the fallen one.

And together, all nine children linked arms
and went toward the finish line.

Of course, all those who watched cried
and cheered and clapped. But the question
must be asked, will we do the same for someone who fails or needs a helping hand?

It may be in the way of writing a letter
or making a telephone call. It may be saying
a word of encouragement to lift them up in
their time of discouragement. It simply could
be giving some money or material things in
a time of need. Sometimes it is simply saying
nothing but just listening.

Whatever it may be, remember, this is how
the Lord treats us. May we, in our following
Him and fulfilling what He called us to do—
being very busy and doing His work—not
overlook the individuals who may need our
attention or our help. Jesus said, "Assuredly,
I say to you, inasmuch as you did it to one
of the least of these My brethren, you did it
to Me" (Matthew 25:40). Jesus also told us
we must do unto others what we would want
others to do for us. Surely you and I do not
want to be forgotten or ignored. Let us be
Christlike in our response to all people.

Everyone the Lord places in our lives, everywhere, at any time, is important. My hope
is that while maintaining vision and running
toward the finish line, we will not trample

over the individual. We must never let a world vision blind us from seeing the people working right alongside us who need attention, care, love, affection and understanding.

CHAPTER TWELVE

Information and Action

To be honest, I am sometimes critical of people who live to gather more information and knowledge but don't do much with what they know, especially when it comes to world evangelism. But this attitude is not always right. God used Ralph Winter and the information he obtained to bring to the church's attention the concept of unreached people groups. God used Luis Bush and his information to bring forth the concept of the 10/40 Window.

One of the things that troubles me the most is the fact that today—right now—we have more information than ever before about every possible aspect of the Christian life and missions. From knowing the Lord and living for Him, to raising godly children and our responsibilities as followers of Christ, you can walk into a Christian bookstore and choose from several hundred books. You can find more information and resources in our world today than at any other time in history.

Yet despite this fact, one-half of the world still waits to hear the Gospel! We have all kinds of information on every country and people group, especially through books like *Operation World*,[1] more than we could ever imagine! But still, the tragedy is that with all this information, more than 96 percent of all the resources and personnel out there are used to meet our own wants. We forget the more than 2.7 billion people who still need to hear the Good News!

There is such a tremendous imbalance between what we know and what we do. I once heard it said that there are over 1,000 commentaries on the book of Acts in the English language alone. But how many churches are there that really resemble the early church model found in the book of Acts? In other words, we are so fed with information, and our "spiritual knowledge" is so blown out of proportion, that we can hardly stand or walk.

It's easier to just take one side and say, "What is the use of all this information? All the information in the world will not reach one single person." But the truth is, we need information. We need the U.S. Center for World Missions. We need AD 2000 and Beyond. We need the Joshua Project and Global Mapping.

Some are called to generate information, and some are called to get out there on the mission field. Personally, I want to be one of those on the field. But I thank God for those who are generating the information, too. The people on the information side of things discover unreached people groups. Now we have hundreds of unreached people groups identified so that we can plant churches there. Thank God that we can do something with the information. This is the beauty of balance, the Body of Christ working together.

One of the greatest challenges for us today is to be not only hearers of the Word, but to become *doers* of the Word. This issue is even more serious when it comes to our responsibility to world evangelism. What we need to do individually, in our personal lives right where we live and serve, is to go out of our way to find opportunities in which we can be involved in reaching the lost world. Whether it is through prayer, sharing or going—whatever way the Lord shows us, each of us must take responsibility and do everything we can to get the job done.

Information without action is like shooting blanks. You know exactly how to load, aim and pull the trigger, but there is nothing effective in it. Information without action is like a pilot flying missions in a cockpit simulator without ever getting into a real plane. Our problem today in missions is there are too many spectators who know all about how things are supposed to be done and too few who are actually daily living it. It's like a football game; there are thousands of football fans who know all about the game but only a handful of players actually sweating it out on the field. We must cultivate a balance between information and action in our daily lives.

Conclusion

Balance is brought through a continual focus on Christ. Imbalance comes when we lose this focus. We are so easily distracted from pure and simple devotion to Christ. Peter was distracted too. In John 21:21–22, (NIV) we find him asking Jesus about John, his fellow disciple, saying, "Lord, what about him?" Jesus simply said, "If I want him to remain alive until I return, what is that to you? You must follow me." This is what Jesus says to us today. "What is that to you? You must follow me."

In all of this, let us have a heart of love toward others in maintaining balance. You don't have to be angry or upset with anybody for having a different view. You are free. A life of balance sets us free—free to follow Him and to love one another.

If this booklet has been a blessing to you, I would really like to hear from you. You may write to

Gospel for Asia
1116 St. Thomas Way
Wills Point, TX 75169

Or send an email to kp@gfa.org.

Notes

Chapter 2

[1] K.P. Yohannan, *The Road to Reality* (Carrollton, TX: gfa Books, 1988).

[2] Roy Hession, *The Calvary Road* (London: Christian Literature Crusade, 1950).

[3] William McDonald, *True Discipleship* (Kansas City: Walterick Publishers, 1975).

Chapter 3

[1] McDonald, *True Discipleship*.

[2] Charles Swindoll, *Grace Awakening* (Dallas: Word Publishing, 1990).

[3] Yohannan, *The Road to Reality*.

Chapter 6

[1] Watchman Nee, *Spiritual Authority* (Richmond, VA: Christian Fellowship, 1980).

Chapter 7

[1] Max Lucado, *He Still Moves Stones* (Dallas: Word Publishing, 1993), p. 120. Used by permission.

Chapter 9

[1] K.P. Yohannan, *Revolution in World Missions* (Carrollton, TX: gfa Books, 1986).

Chapter 10

[1] Paul Billheimer, *Love Covers* (Fort Washington, PA: Christian Literature Crusade, 1980).

Chapter 12

[1] Patrick Johnstone and Jason Mandryk, *Operation World* (Waynesboro, GA: Paternoster Publishing, 2001).

ABOUT GOSPEL FOR ASIA

God specifically called us to invest our lives to reach the most unreached in Asia through training and sending out national missionaries. Today, thousands of GFA-supported workers serve fulltime to bring the Gospel to those still waiting to hear.

To train national missionaries and share the love of Christ throughout Asia, Gospel for Asia

- supports Bible colleges
- airs radio broadcasts
- distributes Gospel literature
- offers education and hope to Asia's poorest children
- cares for leprosy patients and widows
- digs wells to provide pure water
- provides relief after natural disasters

Visit **www.gfa.org** to learn more about these and other ministries of Gospel for Asia and to discover how you can get involved. While there, be sure to order your free copy of K.P. Yohannan's best-selling book *Revolution in World Missions*.

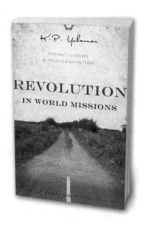

Australia
P.O. Box 3587
Toowoomba QLD 4350
Freephone: 1300 889 339
infoaust@gfa.org

Canada
245 King Street E
Stoney Creek, ON L8G 1L9
Toll-free: 1-888-WIN-ASIA
info@gfa.ca

Finland
PL 63, FI-65101, Vaasa
Phone: 050 036 9699
infofi@gfa.org

Korea
Seok-Am Blg 5th floor, 6-9 Teheran-ro 25 gil
Yeoksam-dong, Gangnam-gu
Seoul 135-080
Toll-free: (080) 801-0191
infokorea@gfa.org.kr

New Zealand
PO Box 302580
North Harbour 0751
Toll-free: 0508-918-918
infonz@gfa.org

South Africa
P.O. Box 28880, Sunridge Park
Port Elizabeth 6008
Phone: 041 360-0198
infoza@gfa.org

United Kingdom
PO Box 316
Manchester M22 2DJ
Phone: 0161 946 9484
infouk@gfa.org

United States
1116 St. Thomas Way
Wills Point, Texas 75169
Toll-free: 1-800-WIN-ASIA
info@gfa.org

Step into the World of
FREE!

At **gfa.org/resource,** you'll find an array of exciting and edifying tools to help you go deeper in your spiritual life.

- Ebooks
- Videos
- MP3s
- Photos

All this and more is free for download at the click of a mouse. Venture into new territory in your walk with Christ.

www.gfa.org/resource